Look Who Hatched!

#3295 Mazes

Heading for Home

Going to the Depot

In the Doghouse

Dig to the Bones

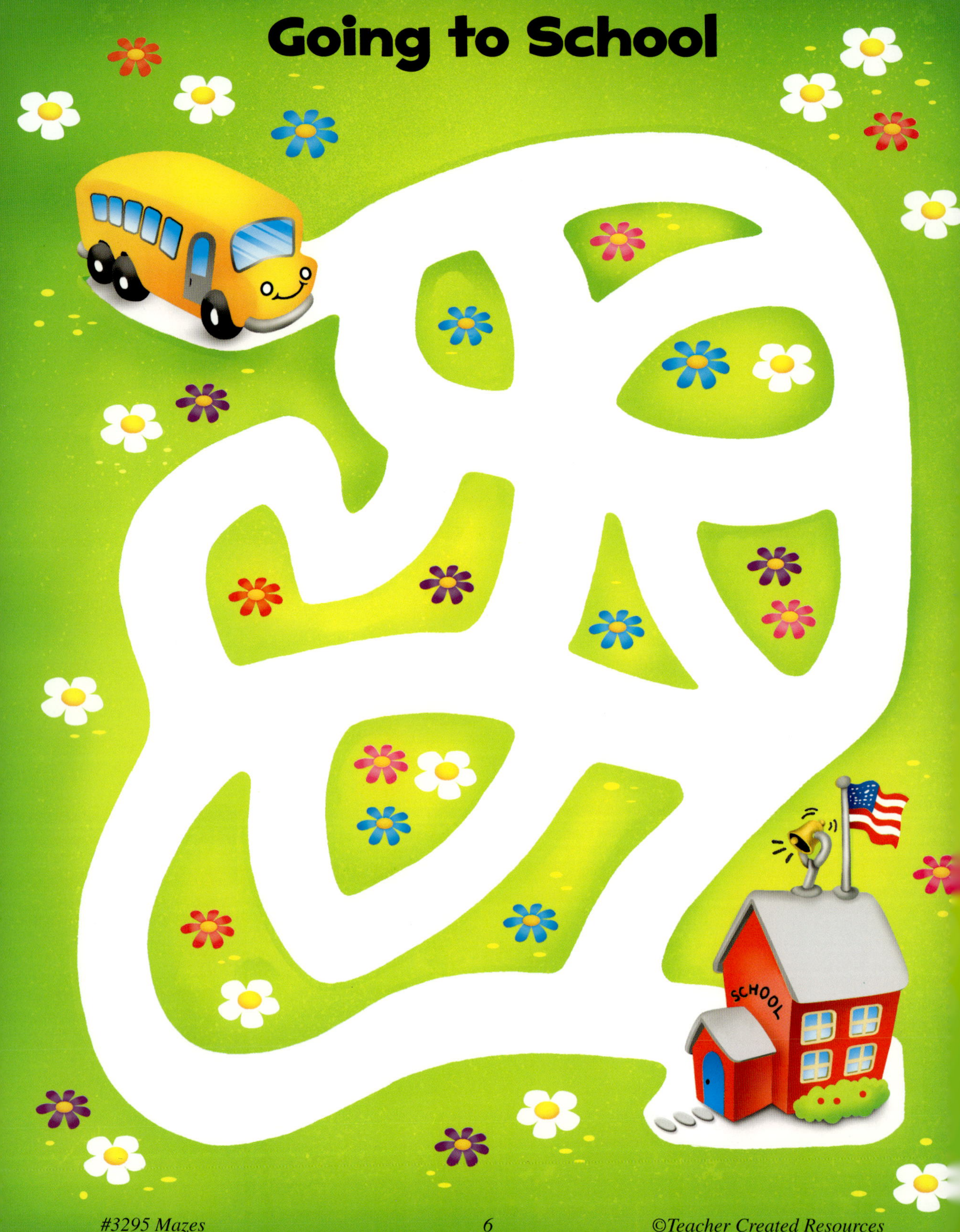

Going to School

Where Is My Mother?

Time to Wake Up

Raking Leaves

Quick Like a Bunny

Where Are My Glasses?

Time for Lunch

I'm Lost!

Feeding Time

Time to Nap

On the Tip of My Tongue

16

A Picnic with Friends

Birds of a Feather

To the Firehouse

Who Got In the Cookie Jar?

Under the Big Top

Watch Out for the Wolf!

Hansel and Gretel

Busy Bees All Abuzz

Sunken Treasure

To the Lake We Go

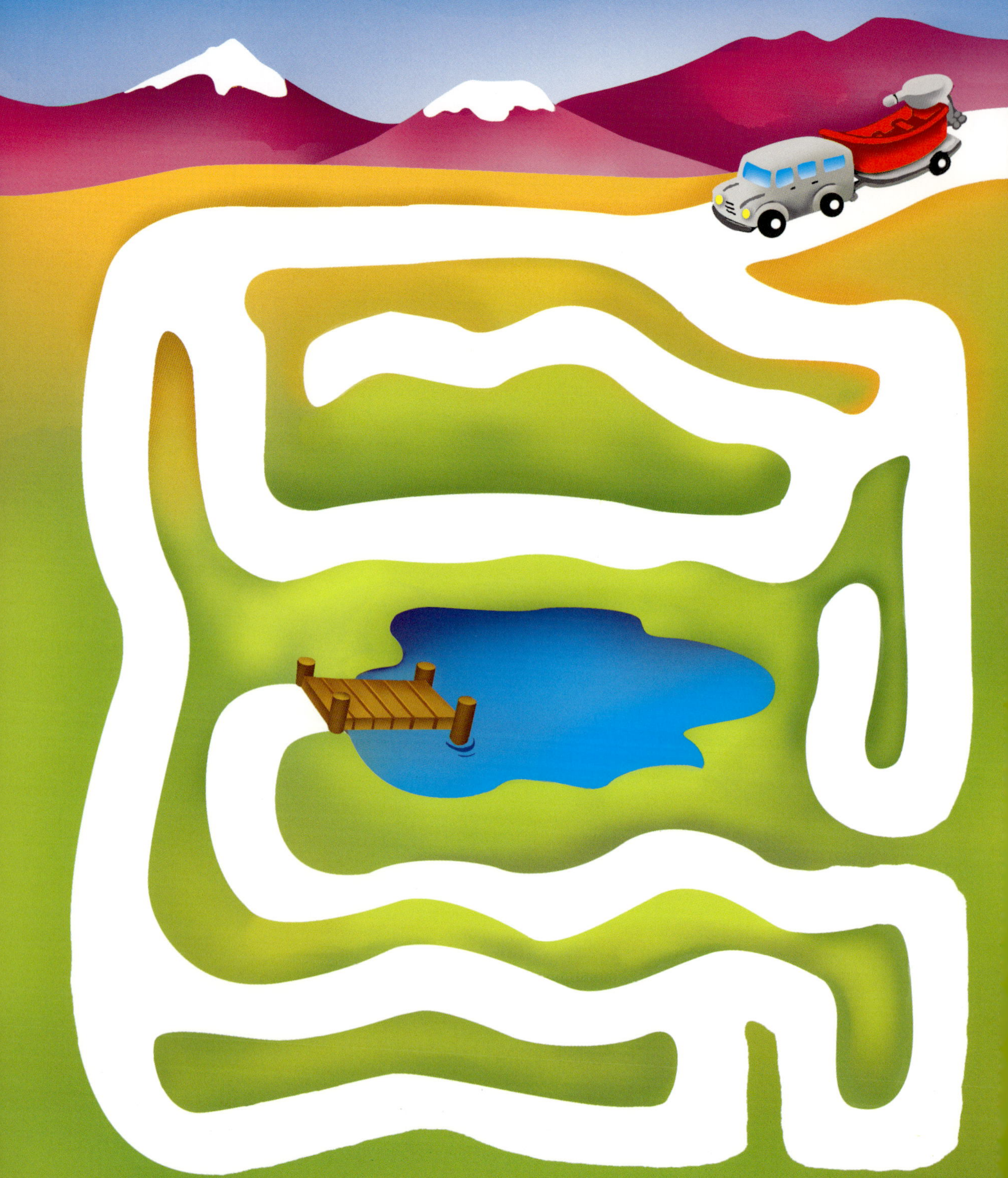

At a Snail's Pace

Over the Moon

Where's the Water?

Lounging on a Lily Pad

Shoot for the Stars

Dinosaur Delight